THE
EASY DRAWING
BOOK

THE
EASY DRAWING
BOOK

BY PETER WHITE

GRAMERCY PUBLISHING COMPANY · NEW YORK

CONTENTS

HOW TO DRAW

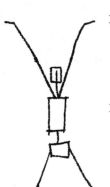

ALL THE THINGS

YOU SEE EACH DAY

AND MANY MANY MORE

THE EASY DRAWING BOOK

A WORD TO PARENTS AND TEACHERS

Children are natural artists. Without any help from their elders they describe simply what they see and feel in life. Sometimes the imaginative sweep is surprising and remarkable. A child will put recognizable expressions on faces, give animals movement and character, and design objects instinctively to make bold and interesting patterns.

This natural approach should be preserved. The exercises in the "The Easy Drawing Book" are intended as a help but not as a final answer to all the problems in beginning drawing. These simple drawings should be used as a means of stimulating and making a game of learning to draw. They are not for copying purposes alone, but are intended as the alphabet of a language so simple and direct that all can make use of it.

The less detailed the more easily understood will be the shape of an object. The easy drawings here may be copied by anyone with a pencil. They are graded: the first drawings are the simplest, followed by the more complex ones, thus making a program for learning to draw in its first stages.

The guide line which appears often on the drawings is a help toward seeing the simple form from which more complicated forms may be made. Almost all drawings are made either of curved or straight lines and many are a combination of both.

Sometimes a drawing reduced to straight lines will help to make a point, as in the "stick" figures or the "square" figures, both of which suggest human form, although reduced to simplest terms.

The drawings in this book are made with a 4B (or No. 1) pencil. This pencil is hard enough not to wear down too quickly or to break too easily. It is also soft enough to move easily over the paper and to make quite a black line.

The child should be asked to observe life around him and to draw with utmost simplicity the things of everyday living. Houses and churches, farms and trees, trucks and cars, flowers, chairs and tables, and whatever comes into the general fields of knowledge and experience.

Some of the many possibilities are shown in this book, but the available subjects are without limit. Subjects should be reduced, as they are here, to the simplest shapes which they suggest. In this way they will best express the child's excitement and interest in the living world around him.

Fun in drawing can be obtained by not trying too difficult ideas in the beginning. The simple objects shown in the early part of the book should be practiced until they are mastered. After the first are learned, the later, more difficult ones will seem easy. (Also see page 65.)

OBJECTS ARE DRAWN WITH CURVED
AND STRAIGHT LINES

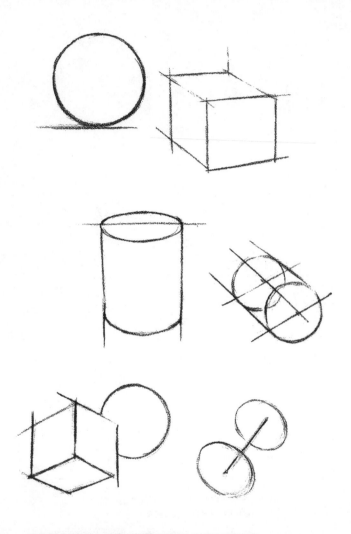

THESE FORMS ARE OFTEN USED IN DRAWING

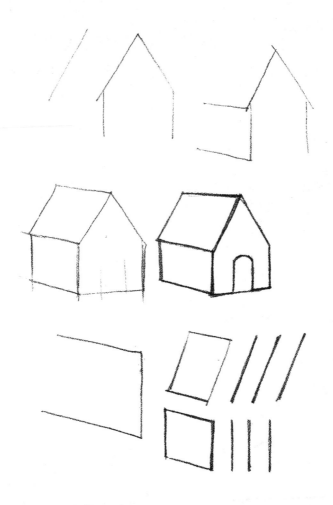

A DOG HOUSE

ADD ON TO A BARN

A SHIP SAILING

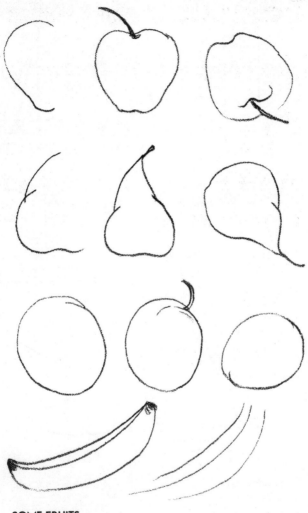

SOME FRUITS

MORE FRUITS

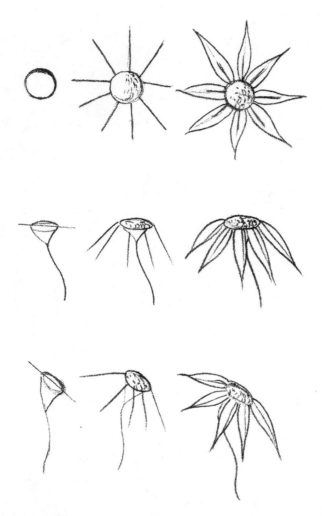

A FLOWER

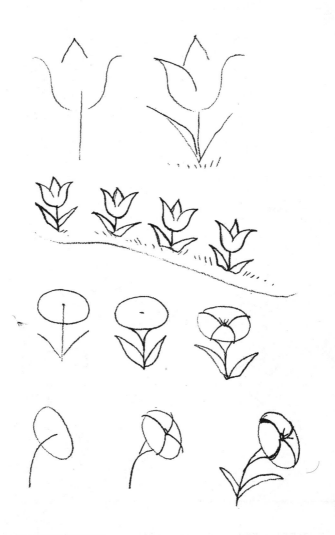

FLOWER SHAPES

15

THESE ARE DRAWN WITH CIRCLES

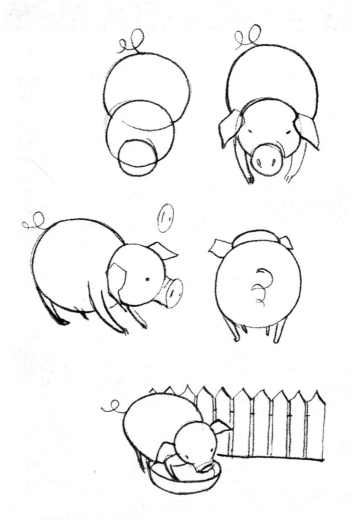

A PIG BUILT OF CIRCLES

SOME BIRDS

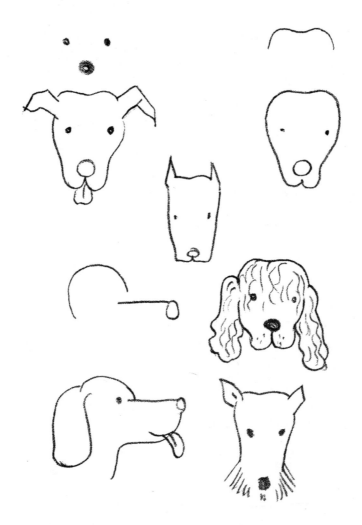

SOME DOGS

A TURKEY

A PALM TREE

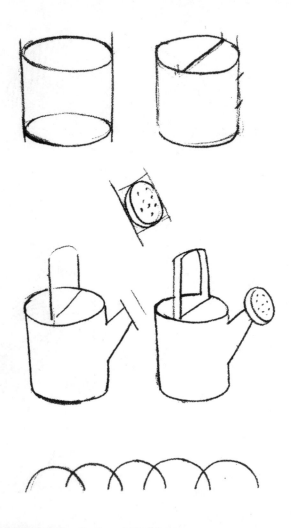

WATERING CAN AND WIRE EDGING

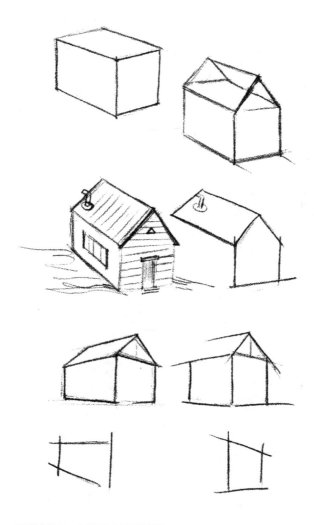

ONE-ROOM SCHOOLHOUSE

23

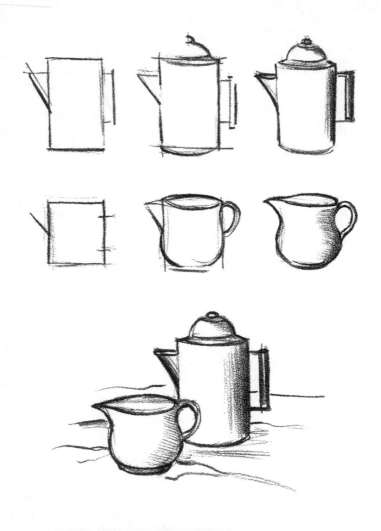

A COFFEE POT WITH CREAM PITCHER

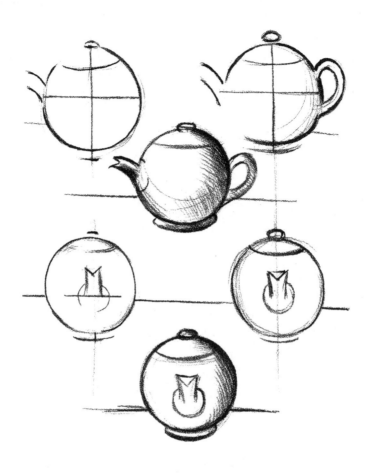

A TEAPOT

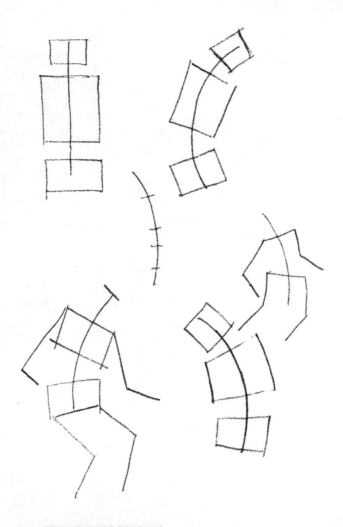

A STICK FIGURE BENDING

STICK FIGURES IN ACTION

MORE STICK FIGURES

THE STRAIGHT LINE MAN

THE SAUSAGE CLOWN

SAUSAGE CLOWN IN ACTION

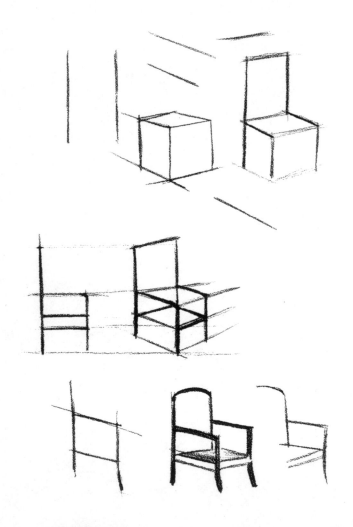

A SIMPLE CHAIR

A PINEAPPLE

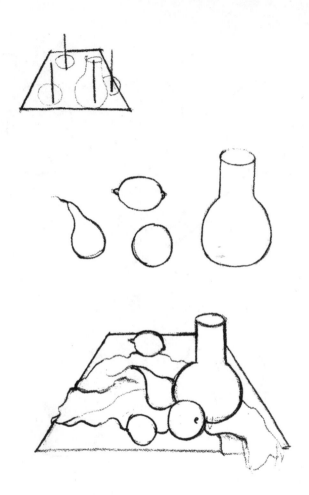

HOW TO PLACE OBJECTS IN SPACE

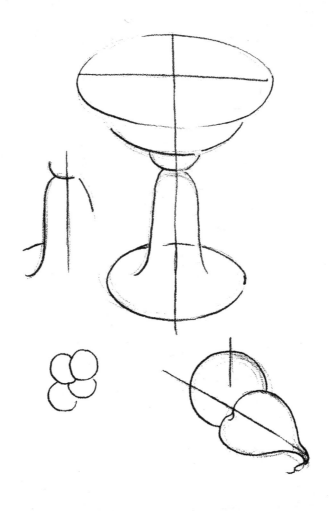

PLACING THINGS BEHIND EACH OTHER

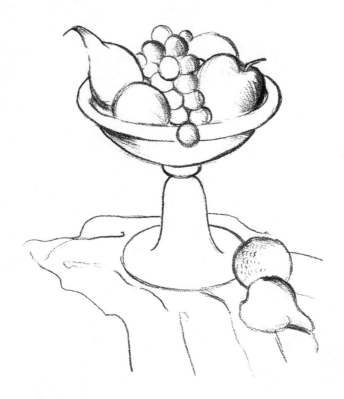

A FRUIT BOWL

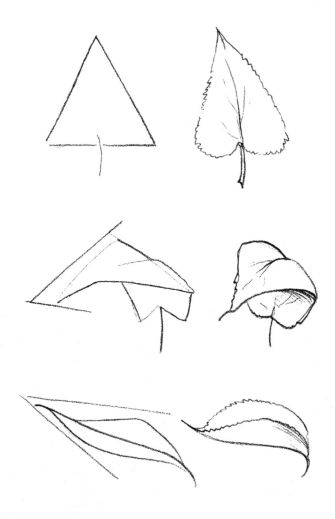

A CURLED LEAF

LEAF FORMS

MORE LEAF FORMS

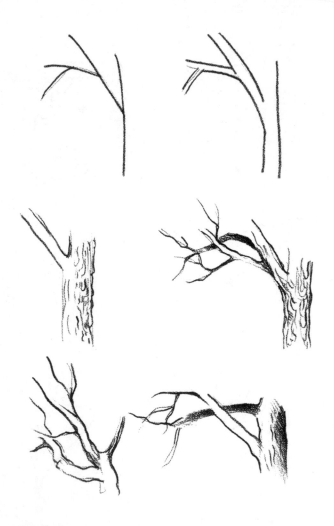

BRANCHES

AN OAK TREE

41

MAPLE

SPRUCE

42

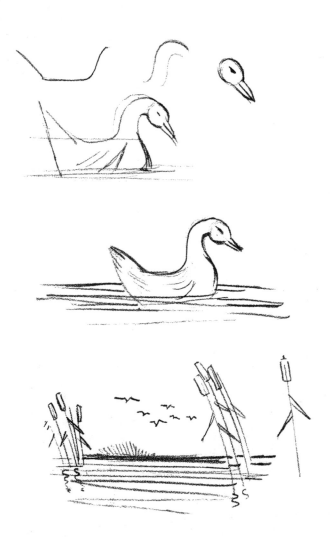

DUCKS AND WATER

LOOKING DOWN ON A SMALL HOUSE

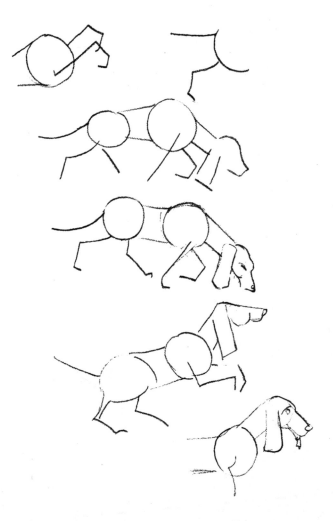

COMBINATION OF STICK AND CIRCLE DOG

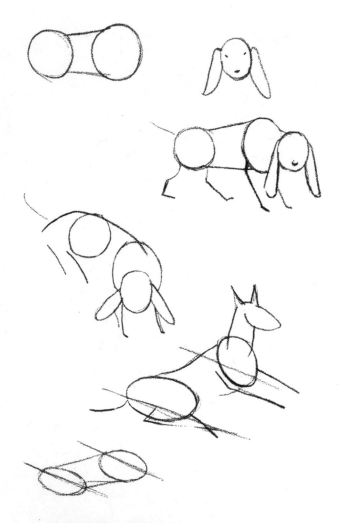

MORE STICK AND CIRCLE DOGS

DOGS

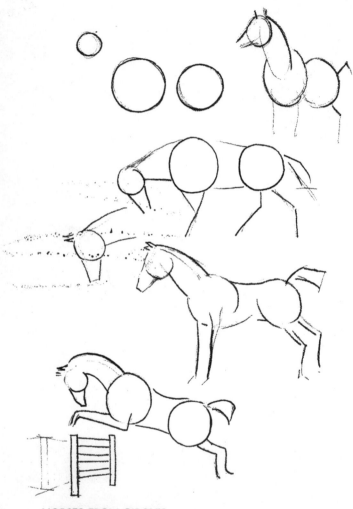

HORSES FROM CIRCLES

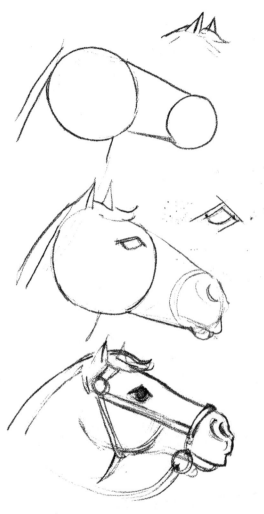

HORSE'S HEAD

AN ELEPHANT

A BURRO

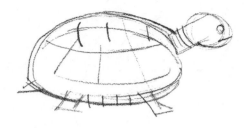

A TURTLE

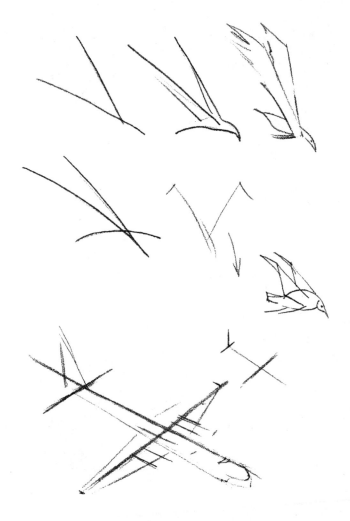

LINE DIRECTION SHOWS MOVEMENT

A SWAN

SOME FISHES

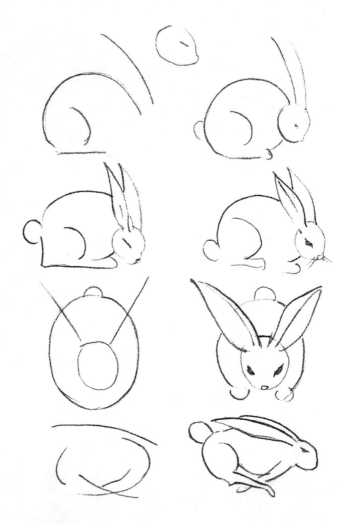

A RABBIT

A SHIP AND WAVES

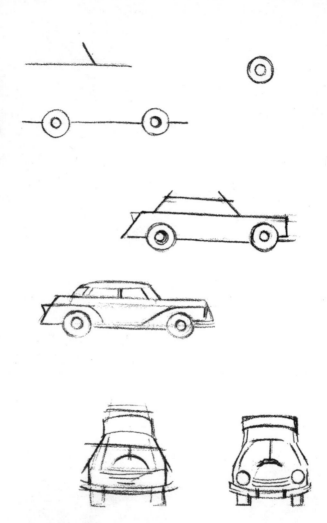

A CAR

SOME HATS

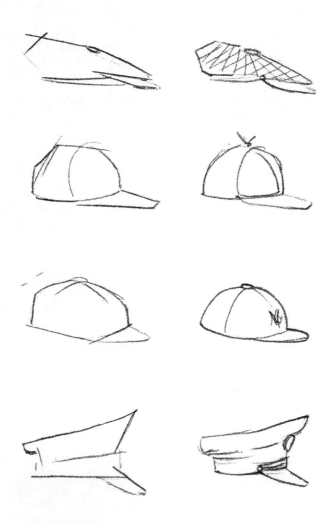

MORE HEAD GEAR

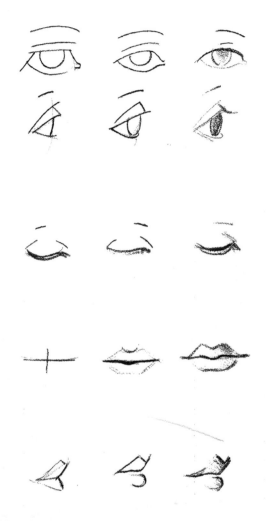

EYES AND MOUTH

A CHURCH

MUSICAL INSTRUMENTS AND BOOK

63

A COWBOY AND PONY MADE MOSTLY OF CIRCLES

THE EASY DRAWING BOOK
PART TWO

A WORD TO PARENTS AND TEACHERS

Teachers of art sometimes complain that "the natural artist in a child" begins to disappear as the child approaches teen-age. There is a reason for this. The grade school child expresses in his drawings the color and form of things immediately around him, the people and places he knows. As he grows older, his interests and concerns are more complex—he looks into things and refuses to take them solely at face value. He wants to show why the train rolls, how a boy throws a ball. But his technical equipment cannot keep up with his desire to express in his art this more complicated set of interests.

What happens? Boys and girls, after they reach the age of 10 or more, become frustrated when they try free art expression, and they turn instead to making stereotype copies of the comic strip characters, or stiff and unrhythmic originals which leave them still unsatisfied — and their instructors even more disgruntled. This, THE EASY DRAWING BOOK is an attempt to help the youngster bridge this gap.

Of course the copying of a few drawings alone will not solve the problem, but the intent of this book is to open a vista, to provide the technique for drawing the type of subject matter that interests boys or girls of 10 to 14.

Since drawing is a language like writing, the impulse to draw springs mainly from the subject, and the desire of the artist is to capture on paper the particular excitement that stirred him. The drawings in this book show subjects that enter into the lives of young people. There are no strawberry baskets and few bottles (the old standbys for teaching perspective). There are instead boats, cars, horses and planes.

The step-by-step drawings start with directional lines (placing the subject and its movement); the second step is usually to develop detail (sometimes more than a single step is needed for adding detail); the final step is the rendering with pencil. Where a subject needs only two stages, only two are given.

A WORD TO THE STUDENT

The drawings in this book were made with a 4B pencil. All you need to make copies of the drawings on the various pages are a 4B pencil and a kneaded eraser. This part opens with a chart showing the pressures you need to apply to the pencil to get variations in lines and shadings.

Start by making the light pencil guide lines shown in the first steps, and after you are satisfied with these, then bear down to make the finished drawings. Corrections should be made on the light sketch, because here the lines are easier to erase.

The easier drawings generally are at the beginning of a subject. If you follow the simplified first stages, none of the drawings will be too hard, no matter where you start in the book.

When you have filled up blank pages with your drawings, the next step will be drawing from real life, so get a scrap pad and carry it, along with your pencil, wherever you go. Jot down at least the guide lines of what you see, and finish the drawing later.

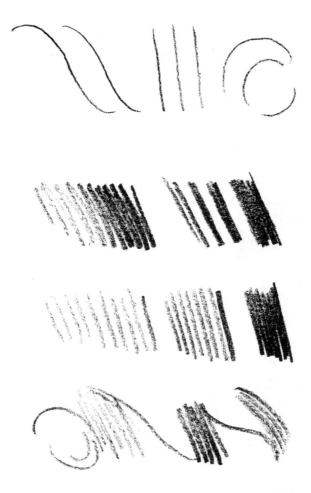

This is the first step in learning to use the pencil. To make the thin lines (top), hold the sharpened 4B pencil almost upright. To make the broad strokes, hold the pencil at an angle. Use more pressure for the darker strokes.

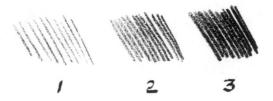

Use three degrees of pressure in the first exercise.

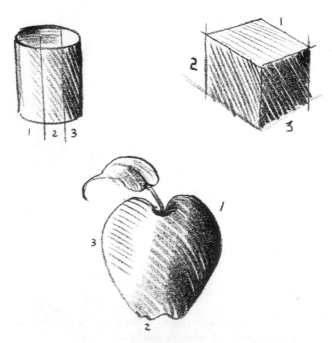

Copy the cylinder and cube with light pressure, then medium, then heavy. The same for the apple.

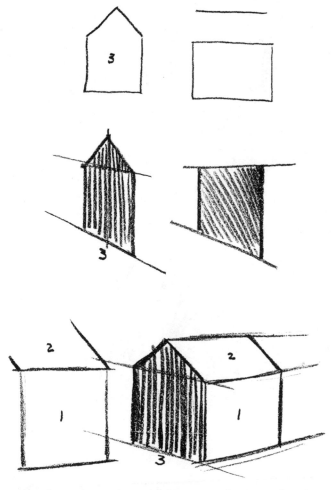

Note that perspective lines come closer to each other as they go back in space. Draw the guide lines first, then draw the parts in the order numbered.

The small sketch in the upper right hand corner is the key to drawing the bicycle. Note the perspective lines. Draw the rough sketch first and then put in each detail in the finished drawing.

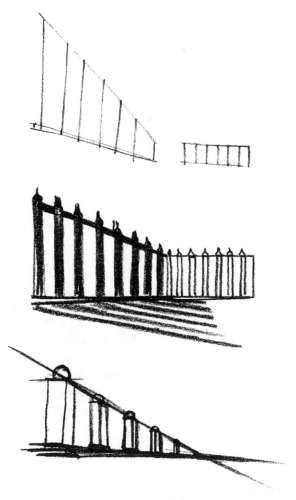

These fences are put here to help you learn about perspective. If you copy the top ones, you have the key to drawing both lower drawings.

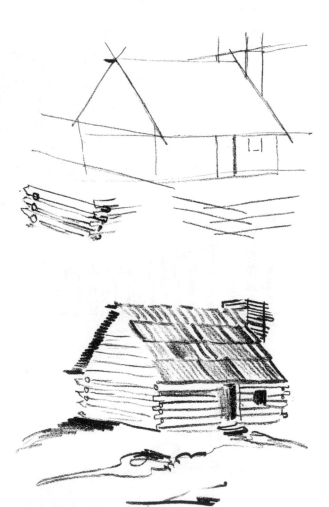

The upper sketch of this log cabin indicates the perspective and the detail in the lower drawing is put in in the same way as on page 68.

This house, too, starts with the simple perspective development. Draw the upright lines first. Then the roof gable. And then the perspective guides. Fill in the details last.

The rough sketches at the top show how to make the general forms of the hemlock and poplar. One is almost a triangle, the other is lozenge-like. Then details are easily added.

Drawing trees in perspective is like
drawing the tence (page 71).   The
trees in the distance gradually
become smaller.

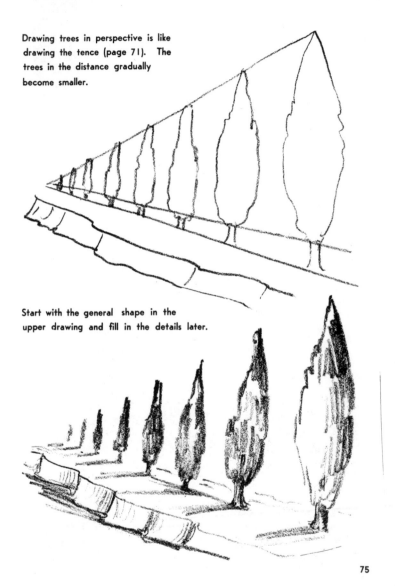

Start with the general shape in the
upper drawing and fill in the details later.

75

By drawing the triangular shape of the tree first, and then attaching
the line of the house to it, you keep the tree in the foreground and
the house in the background. Notice that the trunk of the tree is
slightly lower than the base of the house.

The simplified strokes on the left side indicate the shapes of birch and oak. The details are easily added later. Note the birch leans at an angle while the oak is almost upright.

Two different kind of strokes to indicate water: pointed strokes for
choppy waves and long rhythmic swirls for smoother water.

Draw the triangle first. Put in the indication lines and then make the strong strokes to indicate the pennant flying in the breeze.

The outline of this still-life is simplified.
Draw the fish first, then draw the can,
then the string. Add the details last.

The fish forms are simplified here. Note the eyes are circles within circles.

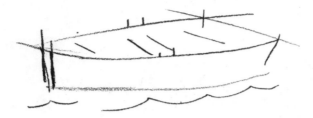

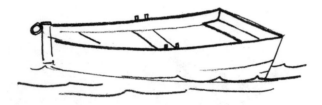

The first stage in a line drawing of a rowboat is to indicate the perspective. In the second stage add the detail. Draw the water last.

Start with the same guide as on page 82. Here you are going to use pencil shading. Add the detail as indicated in the three steps.

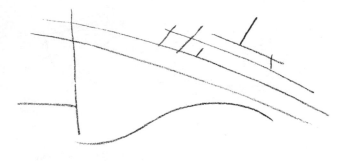

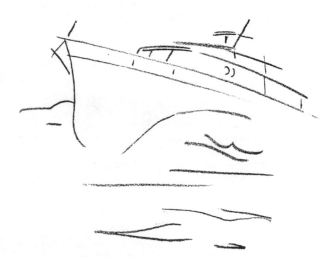

This cruiser starts from a very few lines in these first perspective sketches. The details are on the next page.

In finishing the cruiser, the next steps are to add rail, bridge, flag, portholes, and indicate the water. In the last stage, add dark accents to finish your drawing.

Two stages of a simplified line drawing of a tug.

This is a shaded development of the simplified tug.

Continue the line sketches first, then add light and .dark shading with varied pressures.

Here are the three steps in drawing an ocean liner. Note the first one indicates the perspective and water line. The second step develops the outline, and the third adds light and dark.

This drawing of a schooner
has been reduced to its
simple shapes.

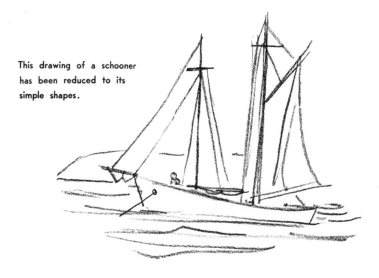

Varying pressures with the side
of the pencil point give the
finished light and dark.

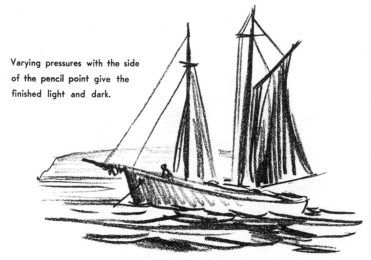

Here we can put the drawing of an old-time locomotive below eye level so it looks smaller. Now the perspective lines slant more. The guide lines should be kept very light and may be erased when the drawing is finished, with all its details added.

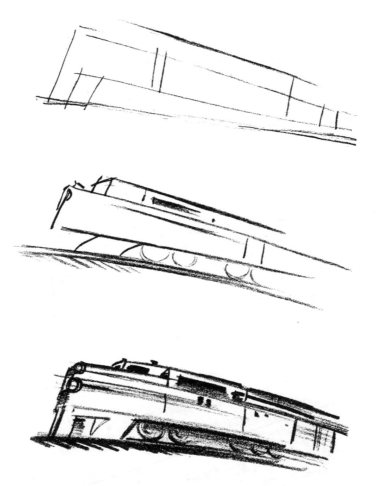

The drawing of a modern train begins with almost straight guide
lines to indicate the perspective. Then the wheels and details are
indicated, and dark accents finally complete the drawing. To make
the train look bigger, we keep it on eye level or slightly above.

The guide lines in this car are not straight but curve to give the feeling of streamlined design.

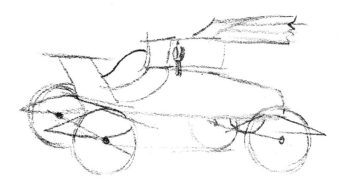

Henry Ford's first car is drawn first with simple outline, using almost straight guide lines. Then the side of the pencil with varied pressures helps to finish it.

The angle is important in drawing the
flying bird. The middle drawing is a
light and dark detail based
on the top one.

At the bottom, four rhythmic lines
suggest the bird in flight.

A jet plane in three simple steps. Notice the first perspective lines
already suggest speed.

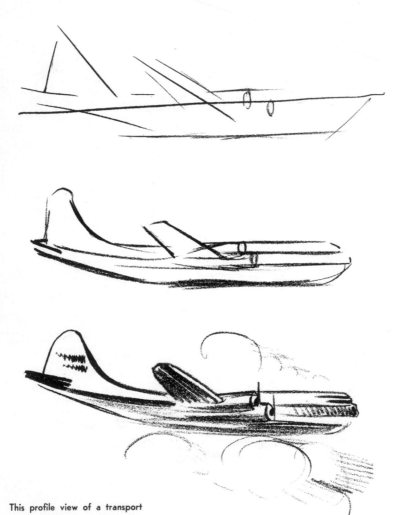

This profile view of a transport
plane can show only two of its four motors.
The perspective layout at the top indicates this at once.

96

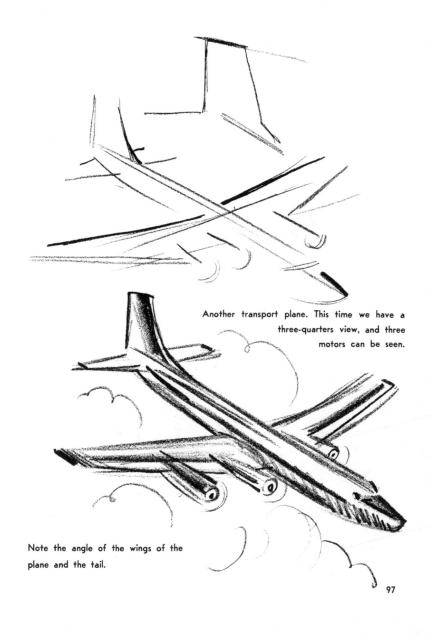

Another transport plane. This time we have a three-quarters view, and three motors can be seen.

Note the angle of the wings of the plane and the tail.

97

A sea-gull starts with a few lines. Light and
dark strokes are added to make its form.
Note its poise and the spread of its wings.

A penguin is simply an irregular oblong topped by a small circle. The light and dark really gives it its character. The beak extends from the circle of the head.

The Old English Sheepdog outline consists of four basic circles with a button for an eye and a gumdrop for a nose. The long hair is indicated easily with shaded vertical lines.

This dog's head is made principally of circular lines. Watch the
pressure of the light and dark in the final stage.

The upper drawing, showing the dog lying down, contains guide lines
to show the position of the dog's body and legs.
Note the circles and how they are used differently
in the lower outline sketch of the dog
in crouch position.

The galloping pony is simplified by means of three circles. The dark
lines show where the legs and neck are attached.

This simplified drawing of a Western Pony is made also with circles drawn in perspective. The guide lines running through the circles show which directions the forms take. The details are drawn after all the construction is finished.

The cowboy roping is drawn in three stages.

First, the simplified form, showing the backward
pull of the horse. Second, main outlines including
the rope. Third, light and dark.

This and the next set of still-life drawings point out how things are composed in space in a picture, that is, how to place one object in front of another.

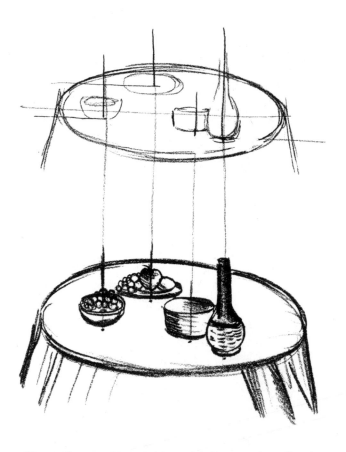

This puts the composition principle to work. The same ideas will apply also to a simple landscape composition. See how the bottle stands on the table, and the bowls of nuts and fruit are a distance behind it. Start with the diagram at the top. Erase guide lines and finish.

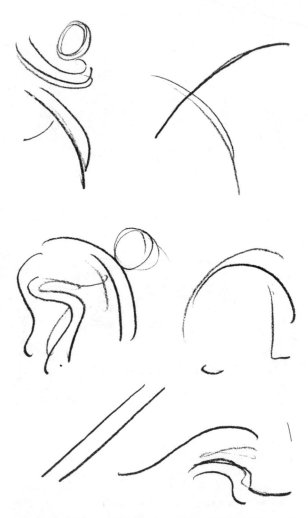

This introduces a new principle of movement. Note that just a few tipped lines and curved lines are enough to show movement.

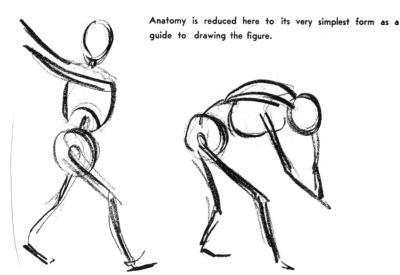

Anatomy is reduced here to its very simplest form as a guide to drawing the figure.

The three circles indicate the head, chest and hips.

A little study of the action figures shows how the placement of these parts and the legs and arms can indicate any action you wish to draw.

Using the preceding page as a guide, you can draw the simplified
construction of a skater.

Now you can develop the skater in three stages.
First, the anatomic structure.

Second, the outline, with the anatomy erased.

And third, the finish,
with light and dark accents, using **side-of-pencil pressure**.

111

A boy skater is achieved through
the same easy stages.

Be sure to erase the guide lines
before finishing the sketch.

In this skier the direction of the lines indicates the movement. In the simplified form, be sure the direction is right, then go ahead with the finishing.

To make the runner appear to run you have to tip the figure off
balance. Draw the finish lines over the simplified form, then erase
the guide lines.

The small triangle is the key to the position of the diver in mid-air.
Sketch the structure lightly, then finish the outline and add shading.

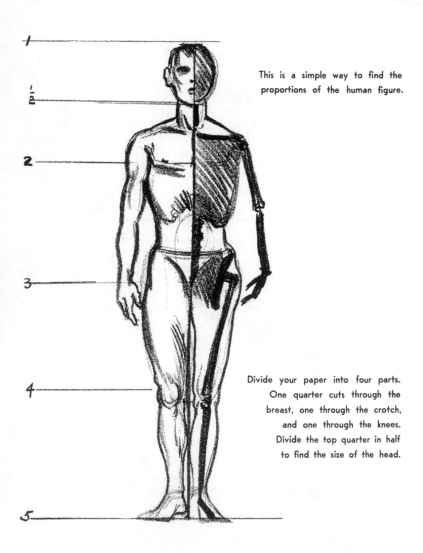

This is a simple way to find the proportions of the human figure.

Divide your paper into four parts. One quarter cuts through the breast, one through the crotch, and one through the knees. Divide the top quarter in half to find the size of the head.

Head   Chest   Hips

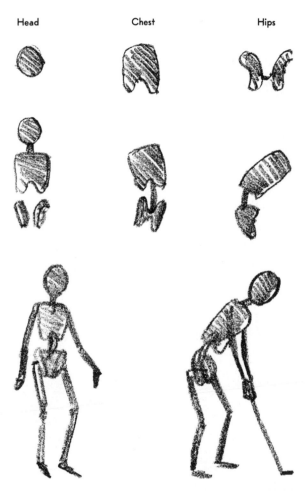

Now we can shape the three basic circles more—into head, chest and hips—and see how the body in simplified form can be made to twist and bend.

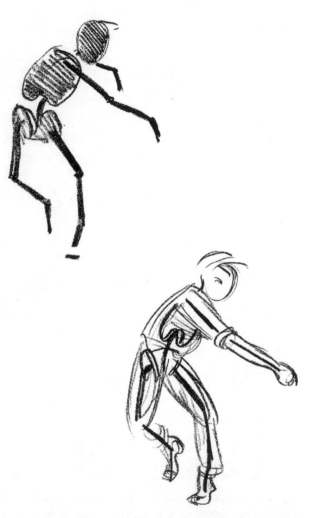

Two stages in drawing a boy throwing a ball.   Develop the final stage
yourself,   then take out guide lines.

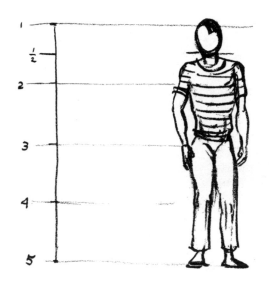

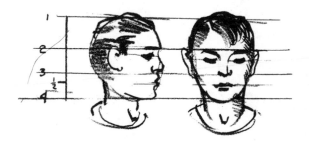

Just as the upright figure can be divided into four parts, so can the head be divided roughly into three parts. The guide lines go through the eyebrow to the top of the ear; the nose to the bottom of the ear; and the chin. Halfway between chin and nose is the mouth.

The proportions are always the same in the drawing of the head. The same guide lines, more or less, appear in the three-quarter view (top), in profile (center), and in full view (bottom).

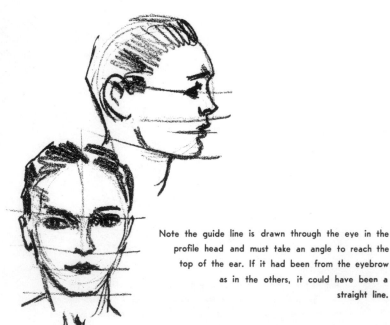

Note the guide line is drawn through the eye in the profile head and must take an angle to reach the top of the ear. If it had been from the eyebrow as in the others, it could have been a straight line.

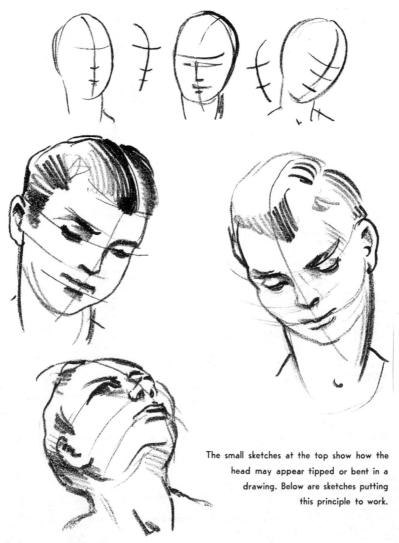

The small sketches at the top show how the head may appear tipped or bent in a drawing. Below are sketches putting this principle to work.

121

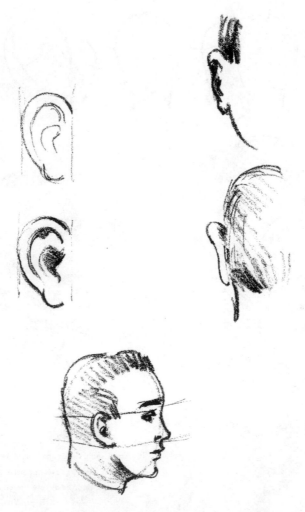

How to place an ear: where it is attached to the head and how it is constructed.

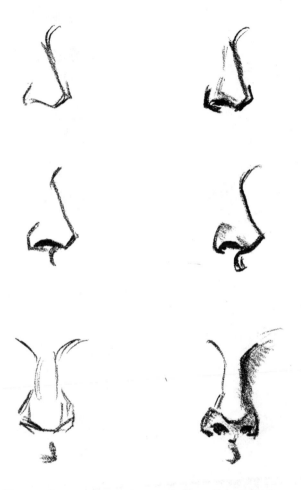

The nose is more or less wedge-shaped. The preliminary sketches on the left side show only the most important shapes. On the right are the noses in full detail.

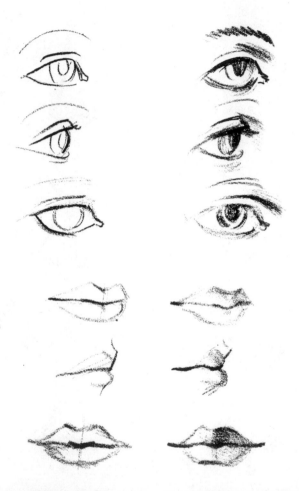

Drawing the eye in three-quarter, profile, and full view, is explained in the top set of drawings. In drawing the mouth the vertical center line has to shift in three-quarter, profile, and full view. It is the center line that carries the expression.

INDEX